The Mississippi

America's Mighty River

By Robin Johnson

CRABTREE
Publishing Company
www.crabtreebooks.com

Crabtree Publishing Company
www.crabtreebooks.com

Author: Robin Johnson
Editor: Barbara Bakowski
Designer: Tammy West, Westgraphix LLC
Photo Researcher: Edward A. Thomas
Map Illustrator: Stefan Chabluk
Indexer: Nila Glikin
Project Coordinator: Kathy Middleton
Crabtree Editor: Adrianna Morganelli
Production Coordinator: Kenneth Wright
Prepress Technician: Kenneth Wright

Series Consultant: Michael E. Ritter, Ph.D., Professor of Geography, University of Wisconsin—Stevens Point

Developed for Crabtree Publishing Company by RJF Publishing LLC (www.RJFpublishing.com)

Photo Credits:
Cover, 17: iStockphoto
4: Getty Images
6: © Jason Lindsey/Alamy
7: Library of Congress LC-USZ62-5513
8: Tyrone Turner/National Geographic/Getty Images
10: © Nathan Benn/CORBIS
12: © Wallace Weeks/Alamy
13: © Peter Arnold, Inc./Alamy
14: Private Collection/Peter Newark American Pictures/ The Bridgeman Art Library
19, 24: © CLEO Photo/Alamy
20: Library of Congress LC-DIG-pga-00827
22: Harald Sund/Photographer's Choice/Getty Images
23: Greg Ryan & Sally Beyer/Photolibrary
26: © Deborah Molitoris/Alamy
27: © Jason Lindsey/Alamy

Cover: A steamboat travels the Mississippi River near New Orleans, Louisiana.

Library and Archives Canada Cataloguing in Publication

Johnson, Robin (Robin R.)
   The Mississippi : America's mighty river / Robin Johnson.

(Rivers around the world)
Includes index.
ISBN 978-0-7787-7444-0 (bound).--ISBN 978-0-7787-7467-9 (pbk.)

1. Mississippi River--Juvenile literature. 2. Mississippi River Valley--Juvenile literature. I. Title. II. Series: Rivers around the world

F351.J64 2010   j977   C2009-906242-9

Library of Congress Cataloging-in-Publication Data

Johnson, Robin (Robin R.)
   The Mississippi : America's mighty river / by Robin Johnson.
      p. cm. -- (Rivers around the world)
   Includes index.
   ISBN 978-0-7787-7467-9 (pbk. : alk. paper) -- ISBN 978-0-7787-7444-0 (reinforced library binding : alk. paper)
   1. Mississippi River--Juvenile literature. 2. Mississippi River Valley--Juvenile literature. I. Title. II. Series.

F351.J64 2009
977--dc22

2009042406

Crabtree Publishing Company
www.crabtreebooks.com   1-800-387-7650

Printed in the U.S.A./122009/BG20091103

Published in Canada
Crabtree Publishing
616 Welland Ave.
St. Catharines, ON
L2M 5V6

Published in the United States
Crabtree Publishing
PMB 59051
350 Fifth Avenue, 59th Floor
New York, New York 10118

Published in the United Kingdom
Crabtree Publishing
Maritime House
Basin Road North, Hove
BN41 1WR

Published in Australia
Crabtree Publishing
386 Mt. Alexander Rd.
Ascot Vale (Melbourne)
VIC 3032

CONTENTS

Words that are defined in the glossary are in **bold** type
the first time they appear in the text.

CHAPTER 1

The Mighty Mississippi

The Mississippi River flows through the middle of the United States and has become a symbol of the country—big and mighty, always changing, always moving forward. The river is a vital part of American history, commerce, and culture. People have relied on it for transportation, agriculture, and industry for many years. The first people to use and settle along the Mississippi River were **indigenous**, or native, people, more than 5,000 years ago.

The Mississippi River stretches from Minnesota to the Gulf of Mexico.

Great River

After the Missouri River, the Mississippi River is the second-longest river in the United States. It flows about 2,350 miles (3,780 kilometers) from its source to its **mouth**. The source of the Mississippi River is a small stream of clear water fed by Lake Itasca in northern Minnesota. The river flows mainly south through ten states before emptying into the Gulf of Mexico. Many **tributaries** feed the Mississippi River, including the Missouri, Ohio, Illinois, and Arkansas rivers. The tributaries widen the river and add to its water volume.

LEFT: The Mississippi River is a critical transportation route for agriculture and industry in the United States.

Lake Itasca in Minnesota feeds the small stream that is the source of the mighty Mississippi River.

Big Water

The wide Mississippi River has been a major transportation route for cargo ships for more than 200 years. Large commercial boats began transporting lumber, cotton, and other goods up and down the river in the 1800s and continue to do so today. The Mississippi River is now one of the biggest and busiest commercial waterways in the world. About 175 million tons (159 million metric tons) of cargo is carried on the Mississippi River each year.

So Much More

The Mississippi River is more than just a shipping route. It is the main source

FAST FACT

The Missouri and Mississippi rivers form the Missouri-Mississippi river system, the third-longest river system in the world.

What is in a Name?

Native Americans gave the Mississippi River its name, which means "great river" or "big water." Today, the river has several nicknames, including Old Man River, Old Muddy, the Father of Waters, and the Mighty Mississippi.

of drinking water for about 18 million people. The river also supplies water to farms for growing crops and to factories for cooling and cleaning machines. Several **hydroelectric** dams along the Mississippi River produce electricity, so that people can light and heat their homes. The Mississippi River provides freshwater for many species, or kinds, of plants and animals. It also offers numerous opportunities for water sports and recreation, such as waterskiing, boating, and fishing.

FAST FACT

It takes about 90 days for a raindrop to travel from the source of the Mississippi River to the river's mouth at the Gulf of Mexico.

Mark My Words

Mark Twain (1835–1910) was a popular American author who wrote about the Mississippi River in *Life on the Mississippi*, *The Adventures of Tom Sawyer*, and other books. In one of Twain's most beloved novels, *Adventures of Huckleberry Finn*, Huck and his friend Jim—an escaped slave—drift down the Mississippi River on a raft. The book vividly and comically describes people and places along the river. It is considered by many to be one of the greatest American novels of all time. Mark Twain was the author's pen name; his real name was Samuel Langhorne Clemens.

Author Mark Twain often wrote about the Mississippi River.

CHAPTER 2
A Crooked Course

The Mississippi River formed during the last ice age, 10,000 to 12,000 years ago. At that time, **glaciers** covered much of Earth. As the glaciers receded, **meltwater** carved out the Mississippi and other river channels. Channels are grooves that rivers create as their water flows over land.

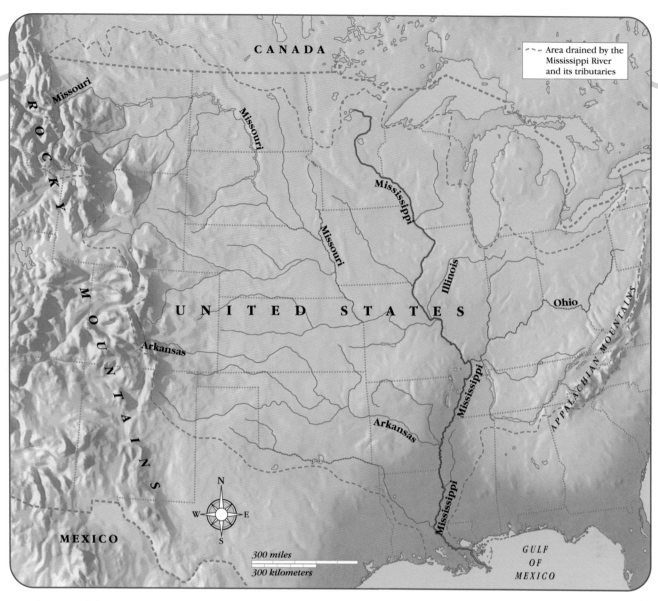

The area of the Mississippi River drainage basin is more than one million square miles (2.6 million square km).

Mature and Meandering

The Mississippi River is a mature river. Mature rivers have many tributaries and carry a lot of water. They meander, or flow in large curves and bends, across flat plains. Mature rivers, which flow more slowly than "youthful" rivers, carve wide valleys.

The Mississippi River meanders through its crooked course. The geography of the river changes as it winds from its source to its mouth. People often think of the river as being made up of two sections— the upper Mississippi and the lower Mississippi.

LEFT: The Mississippi River meanders, winding in large curves as it flows toward the Gulf of Mexico.

Farm fields and grain silos are common sights along the upper Mississippi River.

Down the Drain

The Mississippi River has the third-largest **drainage basin** in the world. Only the Amazon River in South America and the Congo River in Africa drain larger areas. The Mississippi River drainage basin covers more than 1.2 million square miles (3.1 million square km). The **drainage pattern** of the Mississippi River is determined by geological features on and below the surface. The river has a **dendritic** drainage pattern. This pattern develops where an entire basin is made up of the same type of rock. A dendritic drainage pattern looks like the branches of a tree.

The Upper Mississippi

The upper Mississippi River extends from the river's source to its junction with the Ohio River. Most of this section of the Mississippi River is clear and narrow. It flows through rolling hills, marshlands, and flat prairies. Farmers grow corn and wheat on the land surrounding the river, as the soil is fertile. Forests of pine, maple, oak, and hickory also grow in this region. The upper Mississippi River is also home to many animals. Black bears wait on the banks to catch salmon, trout, and sunfish, while deer, moose, and beavers forage for food in the forests.

FAST FACT

The Mississippi River drains water from 31 U.S. states, or about 40 percent of the land in the country. The river also drains water from the Canadian provinces of Alberta and Saskatchewan. The Milk River, Battle Creek, Lodge Creek, and Frenchman River all carry water to the Mississippi via the Missouri River.

sediment. Sediment turns the lower Mississippi River muddy and brown.

Muddy Waters

The Mississippi River often overflows its banks. When the river floods, it leaves sediment on the land. Sediment is filled with nutrients that make the soil in such states as Missouri, Arkansas, Louisiana, Tennessee, and Mississippi good for farming. Farmers there grow cotton, rice, peanuts, tobacco, and other crops. Trees such as southern oaks and tupelos also grow well in this warm, wet area. Carp and catfish swim in the muddy waters of the lower Mississippi River.

The Lower Mississippi

The lower Mississippi River extends from the river's junction with the Ohio River to its mouth near New Orleans, Louisiana. As the Mississippi River flows south, many tributaries join it, adding water. Tributaries also add **sediment**, or minerals and organic material. The Missouri River, which drains the plains west of the Mississippi River, is the longest tributary and carries the most

The Mississippi Delta

As the Mississippi River flows south of New Orleans, it branches out into many **distributaries** that flow into the Gulf of Mexico. The distributaries of the Mississippi River are small canals found in swamps and **bayous**. They form a wet, muddy triangular area called a **delta**. The Mississippi delta covers an area of about 13,000 square miles (33,670 square km). The swampy delta region is home to many species

The muddy waters of the Mississippi River at New Orleans, Louisiana.

For the Birds

Millions of **migrating** birds travel along the Mississippi River each year. The bird migration route is called the Mississippi flyway. The flyway provides food, water, and shelter for geese, ducks, swans, and other birds that travel between Canada and the United States when the seasons change.

of animals, including alligators, frogs, crayfish, shrimp, river otters, and raccoons. Orchids, cypresses, and rubber trees grow in the delta. Rice and sugarcane are the main farm crops.

Flood Watch!

The lower Mississippi River often floods. Most of the floods are caused by large amounts of water brought to the river by its tributaries—particularly

The rain-swollen Mississippi River overflows its banks in St. Charles County, Missouri.

the Ohio and Missouri rivers—after periods of heavy rainfall and quickly melting snow.

Many destructive floods have occurred in the history of the river. One of the most damaging floods in U.S. history happened in 1927. The Great Mississippi Flood covered 27,000 square miles (70,000 square km) of land with water. The floodwaters were up to 30 feet (ten m) deep, leaving 700,000 people homeless and killing close to 250 people in seven states.

NOTABLE QUOTE

"It seems safe to say that [the Mississippi] is ... the crookedest river in the world, since in one part of its journey it uses up one thousand three hundred miles to cover the same ground that the crow would fly over in six hundred and seventy-five."

—Mark Twain, in *Life on the Mississippi* (1883)

CHAPTER 3

Settling Along the Mississippi

Indigenous people have a long history in the Mississippi River valley. Between 700 BC and 900 BC, the **Mississipian culture** developed within the Mississippi **floodplain**. A floodplain is a flat area of land near a river that often floods. The culture was based on large-scale farming of maize (corn) and, to a lesser extent, beans, squash, and other crops. People of the Mississippian culture also hunted, fished, and gathered wild berries for food. They built large communities along the river. These communities included temples built on huge mounds of soil.

Later groups of indigenous people also used the Mississippi River for fishing, hunting, farming, traveling, and trading goods. Nations such as the Ojibwa, the Kickapoo, and the Illinois lived on the upper Mississippi River. Other nations, such as the Chickasaw and the Tunica, settled on the lower Mississippi floodplain. Nations of the lower Mississippi planted corn, beans, squash, and other crops in the fertile soil along the river.

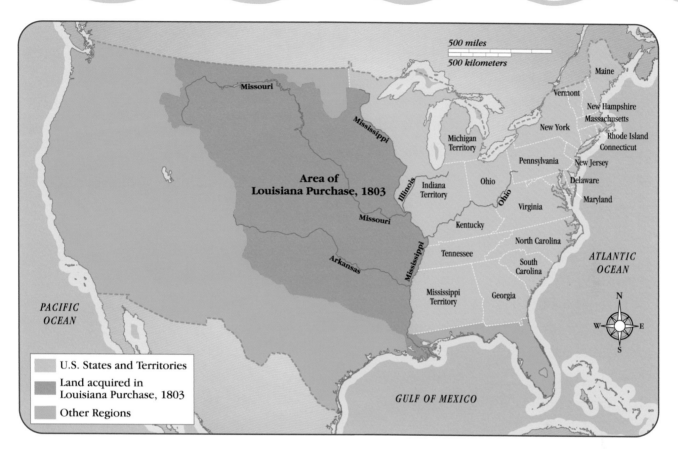

In 1803, a large area of land west of the Mississipi River known as the Louisiana Territory was purchased by the United States from France. The Louisiana Purchase almost doubled the size of the United States.

European Explorers

In 1541, the Spanish explorer Hernando de Soto came to North America in search of gold and a passage to China. Instead, he found the mighty Mississippi River. More than a century later, French explorers Louis Jolliet and Jacques Marquette traveled down the Mississippi River by canoe in search of an east-west trade route. When they discovered that the Mississippi River ran from north to south, they abandoned their search. In 1682, French explorer René-Robert Cavelier, Sieur de La Salle, claimed the Mississippi River basin for France. He named the area Louisiana in honor of the king of France, Louis XIV.

LEFT: As the western United States opened up to settlement, the Mississippi River grew in importance as a transportation route.

Fighting for Control

Over the next hundred years, the Mississippi River and its surrounding lands were claimed at different times by France, Great Britain, and Spain. In 1783, at the end of the **American Revolution**, the river became the western boundary of the United States. In 1803, the United States bought the Louisiana Territory west of the river from France for $15 million in an agreement called the Louisiana Purchase. From east to west, the Louisiana Territory extended from the Mississippi River to the Rocky Mountains; from north to south, it stretched from Canada to the Gulf of Mexico.

FAST FACT

New Orleans was the first town built along the Mississippi River. It was established by Jean-Baptiste Le Moyne, Sieur de Bienville, in 1718 and soon became the biggest city on the river.

Exploring the West

Americans soon began exploring the land west of the Mississippi River. From 1804 to 1806, a group of explorers led by Meriwether Lewis and William Clark traveled from St. Louis up the Missouri River and crossed the Rocky Mountains. After reaching the Pacific Ocean, they returned to St. Louis.

NOTABLE QUOTE

"I feel that there is something in having passed one's childhood beside the big [Mississippi River].... The river cast a spell over the entirety of my life. It was always with me."

—poet T.S. Eliot, who grew up in St. Louis, Missouri

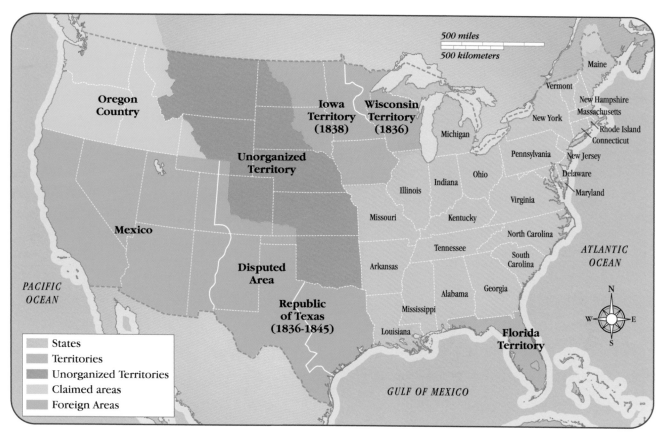

Within 35 years of the Louisiana Purchase, several additional U.S. states and territories had been organized.

Gateway to the West

Millions of **pioneers** heading west passed through the city of St. Louis in the 1800s. Located near the midpoint of the Mississippi River, the city was an important transportation **hub** and trading post. Today, the 630-foot (190-m) stainless steel Gateway Arch on the west bank of the river in St. Louis honors the city's role as the Gateway to the West.

The Gateway Arch is the tallest monument in the United States. It is 630 feet (190 m) high—more than twice the height of the Statue of Liberty.

Lewis and Clark charted maps and wrote notes about the plants, animals, and people they saw on their long journey. Many Americans who were eager to claim free land soon followed them west. The pioneers stopped in cities along the Mississippi River, such as St. Louis and Memphis, Tennessee, to buy supplies so they could continue their long journeys.

Here to Stay

Many Americans who had planned to travel to the West decided to settle along the Mississippi River instead. The settlers cleared the land near the river to build homes and farms. Settlers on the upper Mississippi River cut down trees and floated them down the river to lumber mills at St. Anthony Falls, in Minnesota. They grew wheat and other grains. They transported the grains down the Mississippi River on **flatboats** and ground it in flour mills on the river. In the lower Mississippi region, farmers grew cotton and sugarcane on huge farms called **plantations**. Many slaves were forced to live and work on plantations in the South. Slaves were people who were brought from Africa to become the property of wealthy landowners. The slaves performed hard work for long hours without pay and were often mistreated by their owners.

The Civil War

During the American Civil War (1861–1865), the northern states fought the southern states, mainly over slavery. The Mississippi River played a key role. The Union forces of the North battled the Confederate Army of the South to control the Mississippi River. In 1863, Union forces captured Vicksburg, Mississippi, and won complete control of the river. Two years later, the North defeated the South. Slavery was abolished, or ended, in the United States.

Big Business

During the 1900s, industry grew rapidly in cities along the Mississippi River. Factories were built that produced steel, paper, electricity, farm machinery, lumber goods, and other products. Water from the

Singing the Blues

Slaves working in plantations along the Mississippi River sang about their sadness and pain. The soulful music became known as the blues. In the 1900s, blues music was made popular around the world by Mississippians Muddy Waters and B.B. King.

Waterpower

St. Anthony Falls, near Minneapolis, Minnesota, is the only waterfall on the Mississippi River. In the mid-1800s, people began using its waterpower to run sawmills and flour mills. People settled near the falls and built the busy industrial city of Minneapolis. Construction of dams and **locks** in the 1900s enabled boats to travel north by bypassing the roaring falls. Hydroelectric dams have generated power for the city since 1917.

The Upper St. Anthony Falls Lock and Dam on the Mississippi River in Minneapolis is 49 feet (15 m) deep.

Mississippi River was used to cool and clean the machines in the factories. The river was also used to transport materials and finished goods to be sold in the United States and around the world.

CHAPTER 4
Full Steam Ahead!

The Mississippi River has been used for travel and for the transport of goods for centuries. Native nations built and used canoes and **pirogues**, or boats made from hollowed-out logs. The small, lightweight boats could be navigated through the winding river and carried overland in areas where the water was too shallow for travel by boat.

Trappers and Traders

Native Americans trapped beavers, foxes, mink, deer, and other animals along the Mississippi River for food and to make warm clothing and blankets. After the arrival of Europeans in North America in the 1500s, the native people loaded pelts, or furs, into canoes and took them to trading posts along the river. There, they traded the pelts to Europeans for tools, kettles, blankets, beads, guns, and other goods.

On an Even Keel

Many early traders, explorers, and settlers used **keelboats** to travel and carry goods on the Mississippi River. Keelboats are long, narrow boats that are pointed at each end. Keelboaters used long poles to move the boats through shallow areas of the river. Moving the keelboats up the river was very difficult, as they were usually 50 to 80 feet (15 to 24 m) long.

The Steamboat Era

Transportation became much easier when steamboats began to travel on the Mississippi River in 1811.

FAST FACT

A single **barge** can carry 1,500 tons (1,360 metric tons) of cargo on the Mississippi River. It would take 15 railroad cars or 58 large trucks to carry the same load!

Engineering the River

The United States Army Corps of Engineers ensures that boats can travel safely on the Mississippi River. Corps engineers work to control the flow of the river's waters and help to prevent floods. They remove obstacles such as fallen trees and boulders from the river, straighten its course, and make it deep enough for people to navigate large boats.

LEFT: The introduction of the steamboat enabled people to conquer the current of the Mississippi River and travel upstream with ease.

More than half of all cargo shipped on inland waters in the United States travels on the Mississippi River.

The large, wooden, steam-powered boats enabled people to travel and transport cargo down—and back up—the river in comfort. The first Mississippi River steamboat was called the *New Orleans*. The ship's captain and crew traveled from Pittsburgh, Pennsylvania, down the Ohio River to the Mississippi River and then down the Mississippi River to New Orleans to test the waters for navigation. Soon, other steamboats, such as the *Comet*, the *Vesuvius*, and the *Enterprise*, were traveling up and down the Mississippi River. They carried passengers and freight such as cotton, lumber, and coal. By 1860, more than 1,000 steamboats were operating on the Mississippi River. Port cities such as Memphis, St. Louis, Minneapolis, St. Paul, Minnesota, and Baton Rouge, Louisiana became wealthy. New Orleans was particularly prosperous, becoming the world's fourth-largest port. By 1840, it had a population of about 102,000 and was the richest city in the United States.

NOTABLE QUOTE

"The Mississippi River will always have its own way; no engineering skill can persuade it to do otherwise."

—Mark Twain, in *Mark Twain in Eruption* (1940)

Many tourists travel on the Great River Road, a series of scenic roads that follow the course of the Mississippi River.

Losing Steam

In 1856, the first railroad bridge was built across the Mississippi River, connecting Rock Island, Illinois, with Davenport, Iowa. Railroads allowed people to transport goods quickly over land. Steamboats were used less frequently, and port towns were no longer busy. By the 1920s, almost all commercial steamboats had left the Mississippi River.

Barging In

During World War I (1914–1918), the Mississippi River became an important transportation route again. Steamboats were replaced with barges, however. Barges are long, flat vessels that can carry huge, heavy loads. In 1917, the United States entered the war and used barges to carry supplies needed by military personnel. Later, people continued to use barges as an inexpensive way to carry large shipments of goods on the river.

Low Water

In 1988, a severe drought, or long period with little or no rain, caused the lowest water levels in the recorded history of the Mississippi River. The drought prevented most boats from traveling on the river. The low water level enabled people to recover sunken ships from the bottom of the river.

The Mississippi Today

Today, the Mississippi River is one of the most important shipping routes in the world. Long lines of barges are pushed along the river by powerful tugboats. The barges carry wheat flour, corn, and other agricultural products. They also carry coal, steel, iron, petroleum, sand, and salt.

CHAPTER 5
Troubled Waters

People have tried to change and control the flow of the Mississippi River for many years. In 1879, the Mississippi River Commission was established by the U.S. Congress. The commission's job was to improve navigation on the river and to help prevent floods. The Mississippi River was made deeper and wider so large boats and barges could travel safely. Dams were built on the river to try to control its wild waters.

Damming the Mississippi

The first dams were built near the source of the Mississippi River in the 1880s. The dams were designed to improve navigation north of Minneapolis. They allowed water to be stored in **reservoirs**, or artificial lakes, and added to the river when water levels were low. During the 1930s, 29 navigation dams were built farther south, between Minneapolis and St. Louis. Locks at the dams enabled commercial barges to travel to the upper Mississippi River. Today, there are 43 dams along the upper Mississippi River. The dams keep the water deep enough for safe travel. Four of the dams also produce hydroelectric power.

Levees

There are no big dams on the Mississippi River south of St. Louis, because the water is generally deep enough for boats to navigate. There are many **levees**, however. A levee is a sloped wall used to keep water in a channel. French settlers first built levees along the Mississippi River in the early 1700s. These levees, three

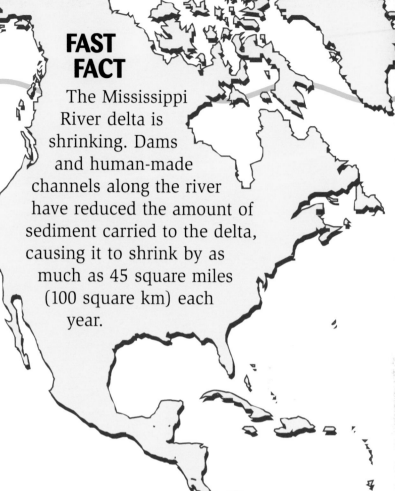

FAST FACT

The Mississippi River delta is shrinking. Dams and human-made channels along the river have reduced the amount of sediment carried to the delta, causing it to shrink by as much as 45 square miles (100 square km) each year.

feet (one m) high, were meant to protect New Orleans from flooding. Today, there are more than 3,500 miles (5,600 km) of levees along the Mississippi River.

The Dirt on Flooding

Dams and levees cannot completely control the rushing waters of the Mississippi River, however. In fact, sometimes they can actually cause the river to flood. Dams and levees prevent the river water, and the sediment it carries, from flowing naturally over the river's banks. Instead, the sediment

LEFT: Lake Pepin, located between Minnesota and Wisconsin, is the widest naturally occurring part of the Mississippi River.

This levee is meant to protect St. Louis, Missouri, from Mississippi River floods.

builds up on the bottom of the river. Over time, the built-up sediment raises the water level, which makes a severe flood more likely.

A Growing Problem

Agriculture can also cause flooding and other problems on the Mississippi River. Farmers clear trees and other plants from the land near the river to grow crops. Trees catch rainwater and allow it to soak into the ground. With fewer trees, rainwater runs quickly into the river, raising it to dangerous levels. The clearing of land also results in the loss of **habitats** for many animals. A habitat is the place where a plant or animal naturally lives.

Chemical Reaction

The **pesticides** and fertilizers used on crops pollute the river when **runoff** carries them into the water. Runoff is water that flows over the surface of the ground and into rivers. Pesticides and fertilizers contain chemicals that can harm plants and animals that live in or near the river or drink from it. People can also get sick from drinking

The Dead Zone

Pollution from the Mississippi River has created a huge dead zone in the Gulf of Mexico. A dead zone is an area of an ocean in which there is little oxygen and therefore little or no life. Scientists believe that dead zones are caused by high levels of chemical fertilizers. In the Gulf of Mexico, the dead zone is more than 8,500 square miles (22,000 square km) in area—about the size of New Jersey.

Carp Crisis

Fish from Asia are threatening the survival of indigenous fish species in the Mississippi River. Asian carp were brought to catfish farms on the Mississippi River in the early 1970s to help control **algae** in ponds. Floods in the 1980s and 1990s carried the carp into the Mississippi River. Because of their large size and huge appetites, the carp are crowding out native fish species,

which cannot compete with the carp for food. To keep the carp from entering the Great Lakes, an electric fish barrier has been built in the waterway that joins the Mississippi River to Lake Michigan. If Asian carp were to reach Lake Michigan, they would disrupt the Great Lakes **ecosystem**.

contaminated water. The Mississippi River also carries the chemicals into the Gulf of Mexico, where further harm is caused.

What a Waste!

Pollution from industry is a major problem along the Mississippi River. Some factories pollute the river with oil, lead, aluminum, or other harmful products.

As much as 58 million pounds (26 million kilograms) of toxic, or poisonous, waste is dumped into the Mississippi River each year. The waste poisons animals and plants. People can become sick if they swim or fish in polluted parts of the river or if they drink water that has not been treated, or made safe to drink.

Hope for the Future

Although the Mississippi River faces many problems, governments, businesses, and individuals are helping to protect the river and its inhabitants. For example, people plant trees along the riverbanks. Trees provide food and shelter for animals while also helping to reduce runoff and to control flooding. Groups of people pick up trash from the water and along the banks of the river. Organizing or joining cleanup crews is a great way to help keep the Mississippi River clean, safe, and mighty.

COMPARING THE WORLD'S RIVERS

River	Continent	Source	Outflow	Approximate Length in miles (kilometers)	Area of Drainage Basin in square miles (square kilometers)
Amazon	South America	Andes Mountains, Peru	Atlantic Ocean	4,000 (6,450)	2.7 million (7 million)
Euphrates	Asia	Murat and Kara Su rivers, Turkey	Persian Gulf	1,740 (2,800)	171,430 (444,000)
Ganges	Asia	Himalayas, India	Bay of Bengal	1,560 (2,510)	400,000 (1 million)
Mississippi	North America	Lake Itasca, Minnesota	Gulf of Mexico	2,350 (3,780)	1.2 million (3.1 million)
Nile	Africa	Streams flowing into Lake Victoria, East Africa	Mediterranean Sea	4,145 (6,670)	1.3 million (3.3 million)
Rhine	Europe	Alps, Switzerland	North Sea	865 (1,390)	65,600 (170,000)
St. Lawrence	North America	Lake Ontario, Canada and United States	Gulf of St. Lawrence	744 (1,190)	502,000 (1.3 million)
Tigris	Asia	Lake Hazar, Taurus Mountains, Turkey	Persian Gulf	1,180 (1,900)	43,000 (111,000)
Yangtze	Asia	Damqu River, Tanggula Mountains, China	East China Sea	3,915 (6,300)	690,000 (1.8 million)

TIMELINE

1541	Spanish explorer Hernando de Soto travels the Mississippi River.
1673	French explorers Louis Jolliet and Jacques Marquette travel to the Mississippi River in search of an east-west trade route.
1682	French explorer René-Robert Cavelier, Sieur de La Salle, claims the Mississippi basin for France.
1718	Jean-Baptiste Le Moyne, Sieur de Bienville, establishes the town of New Orleans.
1763	The Treaty of Paris gives Great Britain the land east of the Mississippi River. Spain gets the land west of the Mississippi River (the Louisiana Territory).
1783	The treaty between Britain and the United States ending the American Revolution gives the land east of the Mississippi River to the United States.
1800	Spain returns the Louisiana Territory to France.
1803	The United States buys the Louisiana Territory from France for $15 million.
1811	Steamboats begin traveling on the Mississippi River.
1855	The first bridge is built across the Mississippi River, in Minneapolis.
1927	The Great Mississippi Flood of 1927 leaves 700,000 Americans homeless.
1988	A severe drought causes record low water levels on the Mississippi River.
1993	A major Mississippi River flood destroys thousands of homes and covers millions of acres of farmland.
1997	Two sections of the Mississippi River are designated American Heritage Rivers.
2007	The I-35W Mississippi River bridge in Minneapolis collapses, killing 13 people.

GLOSSARY

algae Microscopic plant-like organisms that live in water

American Revolution The struggle of the American colonies for independence from Great Britain (1775–1783)

barge A long, flat-bottomed boat used mostly for the transport of goods and usually propelled by towing

bayous Slow-moving, marshy waterways

delta A triangular or fan-shaped area of land at the mouth of a river

dendritic Branching like a tree

distributaries Streams that branch out from main rivers and carry water to the sea

drainage basin The area of land drained by a river and its tributaries

drainage pattern The arrangement of a main stream and its tributaries

ecosystem A complex community of organisms and their environments functioning as a unit

flatboats Flat-bottomed, rectangular boats that float in water (not on water, as rafts do)

floodplain The flat land along a river that is covered by water during a flood

glaciers Large bodies of ice and snow moving slowly down a slope or spreading outward on land

habitats The places or environments where certain plants or animals naturally live and grow

hub A center of activity or traffic

hydroelectric Relating to electricity that is produced by using the movement of water

indigenous Living or occurring naturally in a particular place

keelboats Long, narrow boats that are pointed at each end

levees Sloped walls used to keep water in a channel and help prevent flooding

locks Parts of waterways that allow boats to be raised and lowered

meltwater The water released when glaciers melt

migrating Moving periodically from one region to another for feeding or breeding

Mississippian culture A cultural development of indigenous people in parts of North America from about 800 to 1700, with communities in major river valleys

mouth The place where a river enters a larger body of water

pesticides Chemicals used to kill insects and other pests that harm crops or other plants

pioneers People who settle in places where few other people live

pirogues Boats made from hollowed-out logs

plantations Large farms on which crops are grown, often by resident workers

reservoirs Artificial lakes where water is collected and kept for use

runoff Water from rain or snow that flows over the surface of the ground and into rivers

sediment Material deposited by water, wind, or glaciers

tributaries Smaller rivers and streams that flow into larger bodies of water

FIND OUT MORE

BOOKS

Bowden, Rob. *Settlements of the Mississippi River.* Heinemann-Raintree, 2005.

Green, Jen. *1993 Mississippi River Floods.* Gareth Stevens Publishing, 2005.

Vieira, Linda. *The Mighty Mississippi: The Life and Times of America's Greatest River.* New York: Bloomsbury Publishing, 2006.

The World's Most Amazing Rivers. Heinemann-Raintree, 2009.

Zelenyj, Alexander. *Marquette and Jolliet: Quest for the Mississippi.* Crabtree Publishing Company. 2007

WEB SITES

Friends of the Mississippi River
www.fmr.org

Living Lands and Waters
www.livinglandsandwaters.org

Mississippi National River and Recreation Area (U.S. National Park Service)
www.nps.gov/miss/forkids/index.htm

Mississippi River Travel
www.experiencemississippiriver.com/home.cfm

Old Man River: History Along the Mississippi
www.hoover.archives.gov/exhibits/Mississippi/index.html

ABOUT THE AUTHOR

Robin Johnson is a freelance writer and editor. The co-author of several children's books—including *Endangered Butterflies, Spotlight on India,* and *The Life Cycle of an Emperor Penguin*—she has worked in the publishing industry for more than a decade. When she isn't working, she divides her time fairly evenly between renovating her home with her husband, taking her two sons to hockey practice, and exploring the back roads of Canada.

INDEX

Page references in **bold** type are to illustrations.